Scoring Women and Relationships:
A Gentleman's Pocketbook for How the Game Works

by Joseph Sorrell

ISBN-13: 978-0-578-01563-7
Printer: lulu.com

For *Her*

Table of Contents

It shouldn't have to be this way.

But it is. Dating and social interaction with the opposite sex has become a complex game. It is no longer acceptable to introduce yourself to a woman with a firm handshake, tip of the hat, and a genteel "how do you do?" Scientists have studied the attraction and mating rituals of many animals, but most men are unaware of the social posturing and mating calls of their own species. I too, was unaware of the intricacies of the game played between the sexes. There is a lot of rhyme and reason for why people act certain ways. Is there a reason she didn't call you? Do you really think she lost your number? If you don't understand how it works, you are setting yourself up for failure and frustration. You wouldn't play against a professional football team without learning what kind of plays they use, who their players are, etc. You would also like the flexibility to be able to change your approach when you see that your offense is not working as you planned. School prepares you for calculus and a foreign language, but there is no class that covers even the basics of how to seek a mate. Men are left to their own instincts to try and figure out how to interpret mixed messages and signals. If you don't even understand the signals being conveyed to you, your instincts are worthless. If a girl smiles at you, does that mean she is interested, or is she just being polite? You better guess right, or you'll look like a fool trying to pick up someone just being polite to you. What is the proper way to introduce yourself to a woman? Do you just follow your buddy's lead and buy them a drink, or give them a line? As you will read, you should not be listening to your buddy's advice.

After years of wandering through the fog of relationships, the cloud finally dissipated and I have gained greater clarity into the method behind the apparent madness. This clarity was not the result of the passing of time or the accumulation of birthdays. Some people live very long lives and learn nothing as they go. I owe my understanding to experience. There is no substitute for it. One can read about relationships in hundreds of books, but reading and applying are two, unrelated animals. What follows are my observations and advice on social interaction. I share this experience with the reader in an effort to cast light upon topics and situations that

I didn't understand until recently. The topics discussed are primarily from first-hand experience, and a sampling of friends. I have also incorporated useful knowledge I've gleaned from many books on psychology and social interaction. I've tried to infuse some humor with my humble observations, so as to keep the reader conscious. So it begins...

I.   Preparation for the Approach

Self-Examination

No, this self-examination does not entail getting naked and probing oneself. Rather, this is instruction on how to determine what your values actually are. The confident gentleman has sat down, at one point in his life, and ranked his values. This exercise is educational, difficult, and eye opening. Self-help coach Anthony Robbins suggests taking pen to paper and writing out your values in order. As you develop your list, you will be looking at a blueprint of how you work, and how you make your decisions. Do you value honesty or loyalty more? Passion or ambition? Making these distinctions are very difficult because we are used to just acting, without thinking about how we arrived at our decision. Once you have developed you list, you're good to go. You know who you are, and what's important to you. You are confident in your actions, and there is an air about you that others can see. No longer will you approach women, and be clueless. You have purpose and are sure of yourself. Ask any woman what in a man attracts her, and "confidence" will be at or near the top of her list.

Confidence is Penultimate

Confidence is key to all approaches. You can say all the right things, approach the right woman, and if you don't **exude** confidence, she will smell it immediately and your game is up. Confidence can be gained through experience, but a solid base must be in place first. You have to be comfortable with your look, charm, opinions, morals and station in life. If there is a weak link in your armor, it will surface sooner rather than later. Do not seek out a soul mate until you are comfortable in your own skin. No one is attracted to someone who doesn't like his or her job, appearance, etc. And if you don't know where you stand on issues, it shows that you haven't invested enough time developing yourself or your ideas. So how does one develop enough confidence to approach a woman in the first place? Men are not *born* confident; it takes real work and effort to develop this indispensable weapon. Confidence must be cultivated over many years before it truly blossoms. It is not like nasal hair and table dust, accruing with each passing year. Work must certainly be put into it to before its power can be realized. It is difficult to convey through

5

words how prescient confidence really is. Not only will it help the man feel more comfortable approaching women, it will change how he approaches life. No longer will he be timid applying for a job, asking for a raise, or stepping outside of his comfort zone. Job interviews are no longer viewed as Gestapo interrogations, because if our man can approach and talk to a beautiful stranger he knows nothing about, then, by God, he can surely field some questions from a 50 year-old curmudgeon in an Oxford shirt and power tie.

Building Real Confidence

Now we'll delve into the framework for building confidence. Just as a quality house starts with a good foundation, so must the quality man. The foundation is formed from two things: 1) beliefs, and 2) settings on the man's moral compass.

Beliefs originate from past experience and boarding. If the man was raised in a loving family with loving friends, he may view the world as a nice place. Conversely, if the man is raised in the ghetto, with little nurturing, and he believes he needs to cheat and steal to get ahead, he may believe the world is evil and unfair. What is tantamount to remember with beliefs is that they can, and *should*, be altered to suit our needs. Changing our belief in Santa Claus is a good example of altering beliefs as we grow, and adapting to the world. It is no longer beneficial for us to believe in this mythical figure once we reach adulthood. If we continue this belief, we would be disappointed year after year when gifts did not magically appear under our tree. Therefore, we alter, or manipulate our beliefs to serve us, rather than us serving them. Is it not reasonable to believe that some beliefs we have today are formed from inaccurate or biased experiences? If one woman cheated on our theoretical man, is it fair for him to develop the belief that all women are cheaters? This is debatable, but generally speaking, one example is not enough evidence to form an accurate belief. One could argue that there is **no limit** to how many bad experiences one must endure before forming a belief. Case in point, our man has dated twenty women, and none of them have been "keepers". Well, he hasn't met number twenty-one yet, and she might very well be his soul mate. The expression goes that "you must kiss many frogs before you find your prince" also reinforces this idea. Remaining optimistic, and not being a slave to

6

useless beliefs ("I can't talk to women") helps armor plate your feelings if you do encounter rejection. It is confidence in yourself that drives you to continue the hunt, and as Jay Z says, "brush that dirt off your shoulders." The bottom line is this: if your beliefs are holding you back, change them. It *is* as easy as it sounds. You may need to modify yourself, or your approach, in some cases. For instance, if you wear a wife-beater and baggy jeans to a professional interview, you can believe all you want that you're the best person for the job, but you will *never* get it because of your appearance. The same goes for the pickup/bar scene. If you keep failing, it could be that you are approaching duds...or it could be you. So, make sure you analyze yourself after you get rejected. You might be too nerdy, too loud, or too overbearing, or lacking confidence. Once the problem is identified and addressed, you're good to go. Get 'em tiger!

Your moral compass is the other half of the confidence foundation. The moral compass is formed from friends, family and religious beliefs. Most people start with the Ten Commandments, and add or subtract from there. Others are more comfortable with a philosophical approach. In the philosophical approach, there doesn't have to be a God to answer to, but you act justly because it is for the good of the society. Still others develop morals from a value hierarchy. For instance, if you value justice more than friendship, you might turn a friend in to the authorities for even a minor crime. Conversely, if you value friendship more than justice, you may not turn in a friend that has committed a serious crime. It all depends how your "value ladder", or hierarchy, is stacked. The rank order of your values is paramount, for the order is the governor of every choice you make in life. "Should I buy this expensive sports car I can barely afford?" If you value looking cool or getting everything you want, then you'll buy the car. If you value financial stability more than looks, you won't. It is easy to see how values will affect the suitor looking for a mate: If "fun" is at the top of his hierarchy, he may go out looking to "bed women", instead of "wed" them. Typically, this guy would be labeled a bachelor or player. If he has "love" ranked higher than "fun", chances are he is looking for a connection, or lasting relationship with a woman. He's not interested in the one night stand, and usually this guy has a serious girlfriend or is married.

Most people I've met don't even think about their value

hierarchy. Consequently, these same people are shocked when their lover doesn't return phone calls, cheats on them, or treats them poorly. If the girl or guy hasn't called you in two days, does it mean that he/she is blowing you off? This could be the case, or it could be that this person is totally comfortable having a friend or lover that he calls once or twice a week. If you are the type who needs to talk to your friends/lovers every day, you may mistakenly think the rare-caller doesn't value your friendship. An outsider can clearly see that there is a mismatch of communication styles between the two, but the rare-caller may be confused why his friend/lover is acting strangely when he *does* call, or why she is acting mad or busy. Unless she understands his values (not needing to call every day), or he understands hers (would like daily contact), the relationship is doomed. And this example is just in the area of the telephone! Imagine how many other communication-style mismatches can occur: guy talking to other girls (and vice-versa), guy wanting to hang out with the guys (instead of her *all* of the time), etc. The differences in men and women's hierarchies are the same reason men don't want to get married, and women do. Most men value freedom and fun over commitment. Women value relationships and commitment more. The bottom line is to find someone with similar value rankings to your own. Couples talk about finances and children before they tie the knot, but all too often they fail to discuss value hierarchies. A man who ranks his career above his wife or family will have a difficult time with his marriage if his wife expects to be in the #1 slot, and his career in the #2 slot. If the man is a lawyer, and determined to become a partner in the firm, he may feel that the needs to work 80 hours per week. His wife, who loved to spend time with him, now finds herself alone. Sure, the money will be great when he becomes a partner, but at what cost to the relationship? Parents who buy their children everything because they don't have time to spend with them provide another example of getting their priorities wrong. An Xbox or new car is great, but spending your formative years with your parents is irreplaceable.

Putting pen to paper and ranking what is important in your life allows you to become whoever you want to be. Do you want to be a tough guy, a soft-spoken intellectual, a playboy, a good friend, a good boyfriend? When you set your ranking, you are in total control of your outcome. If you don't like your current lot in life, or how you are perceived, change it. It could be that you're broke simply because you have "fun" ranked higher than "security". So you would rather spend your whole paycheck going out to have fun, and you don't have enough when the bills come. Swap "fun" and "security" and the problem will resolve. Of course, I'm not suggesting only changing the order on a piece of paper. You must commit to the change in action, not in word alone.

Once you know who you are and what is important to you, you can begin liking yourself. You must like yourself before anyone else will. Why should someone invest in you, if you wouldn't even invest in yourself? A man who is not comfortable in his own skin will have a difficult time attracting and keeping a mate. The mate will see something they like in the man, but because his values are internally conflicted, his behavior will appear ambiguous. For instance, the man tells her how beautiful she is, and he makes her laugh. He doesn't tell her that he has a girlfriend though. He has "making someone happy" ranked higher than "honesty", and when the woman finds out, she must decide if she is OK with these value rankings, and if they are compatible with hers. After time, hopefully, our man figures out that his ranking of values causes him to look dishonest, and repels potential mates (assuming he is not happy with his current girlfriend). An interesting point here is that **the key to the one- night stand is that you only have to hide your value hierarchy for a night.** Anyone can create an attractive personality for an evening. The facade crumbles with subsequent encounters, as the other party has more data or material to analyze and interpret. With more data, inconsistencies quickly surface and the bullshit-meter goes berserk. The beauty of the one-night stand is the hookup occurs before the bullshit-meter is triggered.

Location, Location, Location

So you have the requisite confidence and skill to approach the fairer sex. That is well and good, but these skills are useless if you do not have someone to approach. It is akin to being the world's best dancer, but without music. All locations are not created equally. If you are looking for a steak in the produce section, you should not be surprised when your search comes up empty. The same standard applies to various venues.

9

Bars traditionally produce a certain breed of woman. Bars are for hookups, fun, and one-night stands. Occasionally, a long-term relationship develops from barhopping, but this is more the exception than the rule. The reason for this is simple. Bars have a certain lighting, single people are going there looking for something (so they must leave with something, be it a number or a stranger), and most importantly, alcohol is present. Alcohol lowers inhibitions, the shy become brave, and the brave become fearless. After the lights come up, the alcohol wears off, and we are able to focus, the new reality is not as romantic as we thought. If we were to analyze what information we exchanged with our newly found friend, we would find that it was mainly superficial fluff, and the majority of it wouldn't matter anyway because we were focused on what to say next rather than listening. We were so into how she looked that whatever came out of her mouth didn't matter anyway. "You work for so and so? That's great." ("Nice ass," is what you're thinking as you say that). This is not to diminish bars. They have their purpose. As long as you know what kind of merchandise you are getting, you should not be surprised if she turns out to be a flake. Not all girls in bars are barflies, nor are all men in the bar. There are some good people that go to bars that are genuinely nice, and not trying to score per se. The bar provides professionals and non-professionals a pressure-free environment to meet people. It is a place to blow off steam after a hard day or week at the office and normal people (not flakes) can be found there. The trick is weeding through the losers and posers to get to the normal people. This is where reading people and experience pays off. The more people you meet, the sharper your people skills become. Eventually, you will be able to read a book by its cover, and you will find that some people aren't even worth approaching, based on the vibe they give off, or how they are dressed. Is this superficial? Maybe. But it works. You don't need to test drive every car in a car lot before you make a choice. You are allowed to have prejudice without guilt. If you don't like loud girls or bigger girls there is no reason to approach a girl displaying either of these qualities. Efficiency is the name of the game, and we are not equal opportunity employers.

The size of the bar is an important factor to consider. Smaller bars allow you to hear each other talk, and can be a good place to meet people. The downside is that in a small bar, there is a small population of women. If there are only one or two attractive women there, they know it, so this makes it difficult for you to approach them. One reason it is difficult is because every guy in the bar is eye-fucking them, buying them drinks, or approaching them. Too much guy competition. The other reason it is difficult to approach them is because if they shoot you down, you don't have other women you can approach (and they know this), so you look like a failure. Contrast this situation with a big bar/club, and if you get shot down by one woman, no worries because you get right back on your horse and go on to the next woman. Now the hottie has competition from other women, and she is not the queen bee. The downside of a big bar/club is that usually the music is so loud you must use sign language to communicate. If you have to scream as you're introducing yourself or telling a story, you lose part of your delivery. For instance, if you try to imitate someone's voice when telling a story, your recipient won't be able to hear any intonations because of the loud music. It is also very difficult to provide subtle verbal cues because of the volume around you. And if you have to scream in your new friend's ear for her to hear you, you are losing eye contact and smiling. The other downside of big bars/clubs is that there is usually a dance floor that women want you on. If you are not a good dancer, this will not be a good first impression for your lady. To be safe, scout out the women before you approach. If she is a dancing machine, you may want to reconsider approaching her, and find a girl that isn't a Dancing Nancy.

Coffee shops? Bookstores? These venues have been touted as good places to pick up women, but I have found the opposite to be true. In coffee shops, people go there to accomplish something: a research paper, reading a book, etc. It is very bold to walk up to someone, interrupt her, and say something witty that doesn't look made-up. The cold approach can work sometimes, but in a coffee shop, it is difficult. In all approaches, you are trying to be nonchalant in your conversation, but that is difficult to achieve if a woman is in a corner reading a book. Are you going to ask her what she is reading? Then what? Are you going to ask her if you can join her (to read a book?)? Again, this is very difficult. Bookstores are even worse. You are going after a moving target for starters. And most people have an idea of what they want in a bookstore, so they find the item and leave. Are you going to approach her, and say something charming about books? And make sure you don't pickup women in the Self-Help section of a bookstore. Preying on the weak is unforgivable.

Grocery stores are a much better bet, because it is acceptable to pass the same person several times, without giving off that stalker vibe. Make sure you have some visual cues from her, to make your approach a little warmer. There are a couple of different options in the grocery store for opening conversation. You can act lost, and ask her where to find an item. Even better, say, "You look like you work here; do you know where the canned tomatoes are?" This forces her to reject the fact that she works there, and allows you to smile, which signals to her that you were just making conversation. To follow up this question, you could tell her about how you are trying to make a new dish, and ask her if she has had any luck or experience with it. Depending how the rapport goes, you can close with, "well if I have any more food questions, what's the best way to get a hold of you?" If she likes you, you may get her number. If not, try not to run into her again in another aisle, or things will be quite awkward.

Churches are a good place to meet, if you're looking for a wife…a religious wife. The best place to meet this type of woman is not *in* the church, but at church functions or outside activities. Yes, you must attend some church functions. A good approach to these women is to ask, "Don't you go to the 11:30 AM service?" If she does, she knows you noticed her, and if she doesn't, she knows you're interested and just making conversation. So either way, you win. The nice thing about church is that there is plenty to talk about. You know her religion, so you know a lot about her without her saying a word. A good transition from church talk to date talk would be to mention a restaurant, or event you are interested in checking out, and see if she would like to join you. A word of caution about church: if things don't work out you will see her every time you attend the church, so don't burn any bridges.

One of the best places to meet women is at a music event. Usually there is alcohol, so the defense mechanisms are lowered a bit, there is something (the music, good or bad) to talk about, and the target doesn't feel trapped by you. Music makes us feel good, and if she meets you in this feel-good state, she will start to associate you with feeling good. No, it is not that simple, but there is certainly subconscious conditioning going on. If your grandmother baked a certain kind of cookie all the time, you associate that smell with your grandmother. Even if you smell this scent, years after she is gone, you remember grandma. The same holds true for first encounters. If the woman is having a great time at the concert, meets you, and you don't scare her away, she may associate you with having a great time. Pavlovian conditioning at its best! This conditioning can be dangerous if you allow it to be. For instance, if you show up with flowers or a gift every time you see her, you are going to be expected to bear gifts *every time* you see her, because she associates gifts with you. If you one day don't bring a gift, she will think something is wrong, because she has been conditioned that if you are there, a gift is too.

Lighting - Beware of bar lighting and alcohol. Many a frightful morning and scary second encounters can be avoided with adequate lighting and sobriety.

Attraction

Who are we attracted to? What should we look for in a mate? Experience shows that intelligence and beauty are usually inversely proportional. Steven Hawking is not doing Calvin Klein commercials, and Lindsay Lohan is not developing mathematical proofs. This has to do with survival adaptations in humans. A blind man must hone his auditory and tactile skills to compensate for his visual deficit. The same holds true for the beautiful girl. She does not need to have superb social skills or intelligence, because she is inundated with attention, as *it* finds *her*. She doesn't need to be witty, bright or moral, because she attracts men from the start, without having to say a word. Generally, these "Hiltons" have the "high-maintenance" appearance (i.e. perfect trendy hair, clothes, purse, and makeup). She appears this way because of cultural conditioning in our society. Our culture tells us that blonde hair, big breasts, a tan, and a sophisticated appearance are sexy. And they are…for a night, but not for the long term. The high-maintenance girl simply reviews this cultural can't-fail checklist and develops her look accordingly. She colors her hair, gets a tan, gets breast implants or pads her bra, and buys expensive clothes and makeup. What the discerning gentleman should take note of is how much work the woman needed to put in to her transformation. This is important because if you are going to date one of these Extreme Self Makeovers, you should know that there is a lot of upkeep involved. These girls look ravishing at night, when they have hours to spend on their "disguise." But if you wake up the next morning next to one of these women, the real Chewbacca in her will shine through. Don't let her Lisa Loeb cat glasses fool you either. They are very hot, but remember they are being used as subterfuge to hide the real her. She's not really a librarian; she actually works at Steak and Shake.

It is best to seek out a girl who isn't trying too hard. I'm not talking about the soccer dike who shows up at a bar in sweat pants and a T-shirt. If she can't even make an attempt at looking presentable in public, imagine how hard she'll try to look good at home. The girl who isn't trying too hard is usually naturally cute, with some makeup, and a cute outfit. Her breasts aren't falling out of her shirt, and her skirt is sexy, but not hooker-slutty. She has done something with her hair, but it didn't involve a day at the salon or an hour with product and a mirror. She stands out from the high-maintenance girls because she has a genuine smile and is not looking around the bar to see who is checking out how good she looks. She doesn't have the biggest breasts in the building, or the darkest tan, rather she has a je ne se qua about her that is intoxicating.

It is worth repeating that the more time a girl spends on her exterior, the less she spends on her interior. Who wants to have the mansion of their dreams, only to open the front door and find an empty house? I only gamble when I have a sporting chance of winning. Think about you odds when approaching the most beautiful girl in the bar. Many suitors will approach her that night, and every night, so statistically your odds of success are diminished by the competition. Conversely, if you approach a cute, but not "knockout" girl, your odds are better because she's attracting less attention than the hottest girl. And you have the added benefit of meeting someone with personality and some intelligence. If you are looking to score one night with a "Hilton" fine, but do you really want a trophy girlfriend or wife? She will get attention and advances everywhere she goes. Attention-getting is the reason for her existence. These are the type of women that athletes and rich men pursue, because these women are status symbols. The successful fifty-year old businessman pulls up to the restaurant in his Porsche to make a statement. His twenty-five-year old trophy girlfriend is another statement he is making. He thinks the statement he is making is, "Look at me. I'm a big fucking deal," when in reality his statement says to the public, "I'm a pathetic old man who has to buy expensive things to be relevant, and entice young whores with my money, so they'll stand by me in public." Don't be that guy.

Choosing the Merchandise

A little observation will be sufficient to weed out the refuse. Get a look at her left hand to see if she is restricted. If she is ring-less, one of two cases is true. She is married and unhappy, or she is not married. If she is married and ring-less, she is making herself available, so proceed with caution. This woman can't be trusted, but it doesn't mean she isn't interested in a nightly tryst. How would you know our ring-less woman is married, you ask? Chances are, she'll tell you. As counter-intuitive as it sounds, this is usually how it plays out. If she tells you before the "deal" is done (and your conscience is fine), you are responsible for any damages (crazy husband, breaking up marriage, etc.) incurred by your behavior. Don't feel too guilty, because if she is parading around and appearing available, there are definitely issues that have surfaced between her and her spouse, and the couple is undoubtedly discontented. Either the marriage is failing, or he is cheating on her, so she must start looking for a lover or attention elsewhere. If she tells you she is married *after* the fact, you should run as fast as you can from her, because if she will keep this important detail from you, she could also be concealing a crazy husband, children, etc. Our first ring-less woman's intentions were to attract a suitor with the "ring-less performance", but then let him know what he is getting involved with. Not wearing the ring is her attempt to escape her broken marriage. That being said, never trust someone who tells you they "are about to get a divorce; it's just a formality at this point." If she hasn't left her spouse, she may be comfortable with you as a side dish. And as long as you don't get emotionally invested, and are comfortable with this arrangement, all's well. Side dishes can be delicious. But keep in mind the taboos of our society with regard to carousing with a married woman. You may be viewed as an interloper, a marriage-wrecker, and morally destitute.

15

Out of Your League?

A lot of men make false assumptions when they see an attractive, apparently single woman. Their first thought is, "she's out of my league." With this mentality, she most certainly is. There is no reason to stratify your social standing before you even meet her. This is not feudal England; therefore you are free to talk to anyone. If she appears "out of your league" this is because:

1) She is putting on airs to make herself feel more confident, or

2) She is a sophisticated woman, and these birds are so rare they often frighten us when we encounter them.

In either case, further investigation is warranted. The approach is simple: catch her eye, smile, and if she reciprocates, you're golden. If she doesn't smile back, play it cool, and ask her why she's so upset. This catches her off guard, because she doesn't want to portray this emotion (upset), and now she is answering to you, which is not what she is used to. She is used to being picked up on, and playing the dominant role. You'll have to gauge her character from here and decide whether or not she is worth your effort.

The woman who puts on airs may be a delightful person once you cut through the façade. Often, women put up an exterior as a defense mechanism. It is not that they are trying to repel men, but this is sometimes the result. We've all heard the models on television say how they are never approached because they intimidate men. Some women wear fake wedding bands to keep the riff-raff away. This is another reason to be nice to women who you are not trying to pick up. Approaching and meeting women is always a little bit scary, but it should be scary in a good way, like skydiving scary. Your goal is to meet as many women as possible because the bigger the applicant pool, the better the selection. The woman who puts on airs is often very easy to talk to because you can play off of her faux-snobbery. For instance, you can lean in and with an English accent say, "truly this bar does not suit my taste." Or you could be ridiculous and ask her when the last time she went fox hunting. When she says, "never," you can say, "me neither, but I just figured because you look like a classy, classy lady, that might be something you may have done." The take home message with this lady is 1) approach her 2) talk to her 3) make an assessment to determine if she is worthy of more of your time. The assessment is the hardest skill to hone because it is gained through experience. The assessment should take no longer than 5 minutes to make, because she will be giving you verbal and non-verbal cues making it painfully obvious if she is interested in you. Just because she is interested in you doesn't mean that she is worth your time. You may start talking to her, and discover that she is a snob or a game-playing whore. Don't let her interest in you skew your assessment.

If she is the sophisticated woman, she may well be out of your league. You will only know this once you start talking with her. If you consider yourself a sophisticated man, then there are no worries, and you should have no trouble making conversation and holding your own with her. There should be no posturing on the man's part to try to appear more sophisticated than he is, for quickly his jig will be up, and he will embarrass himself. If you are a NASCAR kind of guy, and you approach a successful businesswoman who has lofty life goals, chances are you will be unsuccessful. This is not to say she is a snob, or that you are a hillbilly, but there is just too much difference in lifestyles and education for a connection. This would truly be a case of someone out of your league. As a rule, always date within your species.

Nothing Ventured, Nothing Gained

Men have a built-in fear of rejection. Rejection damages their ego, so why put themselves out there when they can have low standards and never be rejected? This phenomenon is commonly referred to as a "comfort zone," and most people reading this understand that feeling. The mentality is that as long as you stay in your little bubble, nothing bad will happen to you. The problem that arises with this mentality is that not only will nothing bad happen to you, but nothing good will happen either. Homeostasis, complacency, and settling all aptly describe this phenomenon. "Nothing ventured, nothing gained" is the bumper sticker that these fearful men need to read and live. Some men haven't tasted relationship success, so they mistakenly think that it is a myth. Why do you think men are afraid of commitment? They have put up with game-playing girls for so long, that when someone truly great comes around, they think it is too good to be true. The men enjoy the relationship with this new woman, but subconsciously they are already sabotaging the relationship. Is she cheating on me? Why is this great woman with *me*? This is too good to be true, they think. And then, men revert to their primal behavior and treat the woman like shit because this is how they have been conditioned from all past relationships. This bad behavior triggers the new, great woman to defend herself and act in her own self-interest because his behavior is now matching up with all of the douche-bags she has dated up to now. Until both of them put themselves out there and are brutally honest with each other, the sad tango continues ad infinitum. He does something, she responds, he responds, she responds.

Understanding Women's Confidence

It is a fact that the woman decides if you go home alone, or with her. This is the trump card women hold, and they know it. Women, like men, want to be perceived as confident. Walk in to a bar and you will see sundry examples of pseudo-confidence. Pseudo-confidence is the female version of meat-head posturing, discussed earlier. Women don't wear muscle-shirts and gold necklaces though. No, they have a much broader palate of camouflage to choose from. Have a big nose? That's easy, hike up your skirt. Do you have a man-face? Wear tighter and lower tops. Not only do women compensate to impress the guys, they also perform for their peers. The classic example of this is the designer purse craze. Ladies are paying hundreds of dollars for real or knock-off purses. Do they understand that if they have the most expensive Coach purse and a man-face, that they still look like a man (and a man with a purse, at that!), and no guy cares about their accoutrements? They *must* realize this, so it can be concluded that they are trying to impress other ladies.

Another way these women posture is by the way they act. These women think that acting like a bitch is the same as confidence. They may try to not make eye contact with any guy because then the guy might think she is actually interested, and to her that would be a sign of weakness. This is the girl who wants guys to approach her,

18

buy her drinks, fawn over her and kiss her ass. Unfortunately, some guys follow her lead and this further reinforces her delusion that she is God's gift to men. If you want to disarm this prima donna, be yourself and let her feel awkward for acting so juvenile. If she acts juvenile, call her on it. One of my favorite replies to these ladies when they act ridiculous is, "Are you serious? Does that act really work on people? I thought people stopped acting like that in high school." Or you can open with, "You're not one of *those* girls who wastes a lot of money on expensive purses, are you?" This puts the priss on the defensive because you used the words, "one of *those* girls", and "wastes money." She doesn't want to be one of "*those* girls," so now she must explain why she is acting the way she is. The woman who acts like a bitch usually has the lowest self-esteem, regardless if she is hot or not. She is used to men sucking up to her, and she enjoys the power this provides her. When she acts like a bitch, she is exerting even more power. The power that she feels makes her feel like she is in control, and because she has low self-esteem, control over her life is something she is not used to feeling. All it takes is a little puff from an intelligent man, and her house of cards crumbles when she is called out. You may be wondering if these girls are decent, once you strip away the bitch-mask. Sometimes they are, but they are fixer-uppers. They haven't done any self-examination or value hierarchy assessment, and aren't comfortable in their own skin. So you don't know what you're getting when you try to date this woman because *she* doesn't even know what she is yet. If you have the patience and are willing to roll the dice on one of these ladies, God bless you and good luck.

The women with real confidence shine like a lone lantern in a cave. They are comfortable in their own skin, their dress is chic, but not showy, and they are usually smiling or laughing. These women are disarming and can carry on a conversation about topics other than Brad Pitt and Dancing with the Stars. Their conversation is inviting, flirty and playful. They don't start off with, "So what do you do?" The confident women don't ask you to buy them a drink first, and they may even buy you a drink first. Another aspect you will notice in your conversation with them is that they know the "communication dance" of give and take. Sometimes they will lead conversation, and other times they will follow. They do not need the man to carry the conversation single-handedly. There is real magic that is palpable when a confident man and woman meet. They recognize the confidence in each other, and sense "one of their own." They know that they are on a level playing field with their suitor, so they don't need to "game" them or impress them to pick them up. Honesty and a laid back attitude are the only tools they need for interaction.

II.   The Approach

Body Language and
the Approach

    The final factor to understand before approaching a woman is her mood or affect. You should position yourself in her field of vision, the closer the better. Try not to look away if she catches you looking in her direction; rather, smile. In his wonderful book, *How to Win Friends and Influence People*, one of Dale Carnegie's tactics to win friends is simply to "smile." Smiling is contagious, and you can change a person's mood instantly with just a smile. Do not give her a Jeffrey Dahmer-staredown, but a simple, disarming smile will do the trick. This is non-aggressive and gives her an opportunity to respond. She will smile back or turn away. Neither of her actions means anything absolutely. She may smile back to be friendly and have no interest in you at all. Or, she may smile back wanting you to approach her, but when you start talking she wants to kill herself. In the same vein, if she doesn't return your smile and turns away, she may find you repulsive, or she may not understand body language. And there is always the possibility that she is just playing hard to get. If she is just shy or inexperienced with body language, she may need some prodding or encouragement. Once you approach her, you'll discover this very quickly. Pursuing girls playing hard to get is not for me and seems childish. Why waste my time trying to crack a nut, when there are plenty of the shell-less variety available? If you are interested in the hard to get girls, make sure your car has plenty of cargo room because they come with emotional baggage. These girls are more interested in their ego and how others perceive them. They would rather look "cool" to their friends and strangers than have an honest conversation with someone showing interest in them. These are the same girls who wait for two or three days before returning a guy's phone call just because one of their magazines or girlfriends tells them to. They want to be the center of attention, told how pretty they are, how cute their clothes are, and how trendy their hairstyle is. If you happen to be blind to the physical warning signs this shell of a person broadcasts, a very short conversation with her should set you straight. She won't volunteer opinions or feelings openly. Rather, she'll wait to see your angle or feelings on something and then mimic it. She won't have an original idea, because she's never actually had one.

The smart money is on the girl who returns your smile. Her smile shows that she is at the very least polite, and at best, interested. If you are going to send her a drink, be sure to check the level of her drink first. There is nothing stupider than sending a drink over to a girl who already has a full drink. She doesn't want to look like Double- Fisting Debby, and you don't want to look like you're trying to get her drunk. I've found that it's best to start talking to the woman first, and if you like her, then buy her a drink. This saves you guesswork on her drink and saves you from wasting your money on someone who turns out to be a dud. And no, gentleman, rufies are never an acceptable back-up plan.

The Pick-up Line

A classic example of the disconnect between knowledge and application is the notorious, "pick-up line." Pick-up lines are meat-head and jag-off fodder. The guys using pick-up lines are the same guys with their imitation gold chains hanging over their under-sized black T-shirts at the Roxburyesque nightclubs. They are bronzed, buffed, gelled and reporting for duty. So now they look like a Ken doll, but Ken doesn't speak. No worries, because there are some totally cool lines they've picked up out of Maxim which should do the trick. These guys would term themselves, "pussy killers." This description sounds satirical, but if you ask an attractive woman, she will tell you she has been approached with at least one scripted, cheesy line. If she hasn't been approached with a line, she may not be hanging out in the proper meat market or worse yet, she may look like a Velociraptor. Scripted, hackneyed lines usually don't work. An innocuous, original opening line is a good start, but that is only a knock on the door. When she answers the door, you must not be caught flat-footed and retarded-mouthed. Some opening lines can be effective conversation starters, when in the right hands. We will revisit the opening line a little bit later. However, even with a good approach, these lines are destined to fail, if certain principles are not followed. Case in point: approaching a woman who is married, taken, or not in the mood to be approached. These cases will be visited later.

The Cold Approach

The more experienced man can try the cold approach. The cold approach is a great surprise and ego-booster for the recipient. Remember that you might see your soul mate before she sees you, and if you keep waiting for an invitation from her, you may miss out. This technique is not for the faint of heart and is reserved for the veteran, because the odds of rejection are much greater. He needs to be quick about his wits, so as to not look like an ass if rejection occurs. For the uninitiated, the cold approach is approaching a woman who is demonstrating uninviting body language or no visual welcoming. Uninviting body language is usually accurate, but sometimes a woman doesn't know she's giving it off. This can be used as a great icebreaker, such as asking her "who stole your ball?" or "why are you so mad?" This must be done tactfully and with a smile, because you don't want her to think you are teasing or making fun of her in a mean way. This line also needs to be followed with a friendly, inviting line like, "my name is ---" or "can I buy you a drink to cheer you up?" It will get her talking...or she'll tell you to get lost. If she does so politely, be a gentleman and move on. If she acts like a bitch, you should remind her that she's not as special as she thinks, and will probably have a miserable life because she's a miserable person. This may sound harsh, but it serves two purposes: 1) it shows that you won't be taken for granted, and are confident with yourself and 2) it serves as a wake-up call to her, that she is acting inappropriately. There is no need for one person to be disrespectful to another, and your excoriation to her retort should make you feel great, even in the face of rejection. You can start to look at those that have rejected you, and smile, knowing that they were not the right person for you. If the veteran can draw this positive conclusion from rejection, there is no longer shame in rejection, but instead, gratefulness. The veteran is grateful that he has one less mate to evaluate, and is one person closer to finding Miss Right.

Rejection

A few words on rejection: If you read the biographies of Thomas Edison, Benjamin Franklin, Abraham Lincoln, and countless other greats, you will find a common thread. All of these great men succeeded *because* of rejection. When Edison was being teased for failing so many times at trying to invent a light bulb, his reply was something like, "I have not failed. I have just found 10,000 ways that don't work". It is all a matter of spin, perspective, or re-framing, whichever term you like to use. These men had vision. They knew where they wanted to be and kept at it until they got there. With each new attempt they did not anticipate failure, nor with each rejection did they become deterred. When a child is learning how to ride a bike, inevitably he falls. Repeatedly. Can you imagine what would happen if he thought he should give up trying to ride because of his many "failures"? He would never ride a bike! Most of the time, we can learn from our rejections. Either our approach is wrong, or we're approaching the wrong kind of person. Some rejections will remain a mystery. We've said everything right; she enjoyed our company, and all of the sudden she drops off the face of the earth (more on this girl later). After analyzing our behavior, if we can't figure out what caused the disconnect, we must forget it and dwell on it no more. Nothing worthwhile will be accomplished by second-guessing ourselves. Move on. There are thousands of other people to meet out there.

When to First Call

The time to first call is whenever you feel like it is the appropriate time to call. Three day rules are out, if they ever existed. Why play games? If you *do* follow the custom of waiting a day or two to initially call the woman, texting is a great way to bridge the gap over those 1-2 days of silence. The importance of text messaging cannot be overstated. Text something cute or clever, but nothing overt. This allows her to see more of you through your writing, and allows her to respond or formulate a response on her own time. If you call too soon, you may not be able to carry on a conversation, and silence is awkward. Texting later in the relationship is important too. It is equivalent to leaving a cute note on the fridge or a short letter for her to find. When she opens her phone, she has a little gift awaiting her. She may be busy at work or school, and voicemail can't be checked subtly (in class or a meeting). But when they get a quick break, they can read your message and shoot a reply back without having to talk in public.

Make sure you make your communication expectations known within the first few weeks of the relationship. If you are always the one calling her and she never calls you (and you don't like this), gently tell her "hey, you never call me." If you are afraid to tell her how you feel, it is going to be a long relationship, and she will never know what you want. You need to feel her communication style out. One girl I met exchanged text messages with me for a few days, and when I texted her to see if she was available for dinner the following night, she was shocked that I asked her out through text (versus calling). But with another girl, this is how we would communicate if we were too busy at work to talk. Another girl I opened the car door for and she thought this was chivalrous, while a different girl asked me not to do that. So everyone is different. Another lesson I've learned is that everyone with a cell phone does not have text messaging. I sent a girl text messages for 2 days without a response from her. I though I said something to make her mad. When I finally caught up with her, two days later, I found out she didn't have text messaging. Mystery solved.

The First Date

The first date should be during a weekday whenever possible. This gives both parties an easy escape: they have work or school the next morning. When you meet your lady for the second time (first date) she may be totally different than what you remembered from a few nights earlier. She may look like a goblin, or have an annoying feature you glossed over initially. Never go to a movie theater unless you want to sit in silence next to your date for two hours. The first date should be an inexpensive dinner or involve some activity (canoeing, rock climbing) that allows for conversation. Never take a lady to an expensive restaurant in the first few dates. Women like nice restaurants but they are not prostitutes and spending more money on them guarantees nothing. You may decide by date number three that you don't like this lady, so why would you spend a lot of money on her early in the courting? As far as paying for the bill, it's your call. I am a traditionalist, and always pick up the bill if I initiated the date. Some people are more comfortable splitting the bill, but I think this looks cheap. You have invited the woman out, so the least you can do is pay for her meal.

Make sure you have two or three interesting things to talk about at dinner. This is a lot easier than trying to make small talk off the cuff. Without turning it into an interrogation, you need to ask her questions about herself. Be sure to remember her responses, so you can rattle them off a week from now, or reference them in a text. She will be flattered that you listened and remembered. People like to talk about themselves and it is your job to draw them out. Mention her name in conversation as well, because people like to hear their own name spoken, and it personalizes the conversation. Be careful not to brag on yourself. If you are really that great, she will be smart enough to figure out how well you are doing, or how smart and confident you are.

Blind Date Guidelines

There is only one tried and true rule to blind dates. And it is: Under no circumstances should you agree to a blind date. This is a fool's errand, suicide, and on par with water boarding, to put it politely. Nothing good can come from blind dating. Let's look at why. First of all, if the girl is attractive, smart, funny, etc, why would she need someone to set her up? The same goes for the guy, of course. Maybe they're just shy, you ask? No. Even shy girls get approached and give their numbers eventually. So the only explanation for why a girl needs to be set up is that she is repugnant in one of the following departments: looks or social grace. Smarts really don't come into play for a female. Guys are not looking for someone to help them with their math homework. They are looking for a conquest, or a fun adventure. So let's assume you had a frontal lobotomy, and agreed to meet up with your blind date. Unless you're a dick, you're going to end up paying for the meal or drinks. And now you're faced with spending a reasonable amount of time with your date. It wouldn't look quite right, if after 5 minutes and 2 drinks of your beer, you said, "see you later, I've gotta go." Of course there should be an exit strategy in place before you even arrive, but you must show some courtesy and respect to your date.

There are two kinds of blind dates: bad and worse. From years of field experience, I've learned that bad comes from a friend setting you up, and worse come from your mother setting you up. Friends, at least know a little bit of your taste, and won't set you up with a troll. Of course, they are still always off mark with their pairing, but they are better than your mother's pick. Mothers will pick wholesome, boring girls without much regard for **your** taste. This is not to impugn mothers, for how could they know your taste? Usually, your mother is not in your posse, and you don't share with her that you like a tight ass and a great rack on your women.

If you are unfortunate enough to be trapped in a blind date, you should use it as a learning experience. One of the skills I learned from blind dates was how to lie, and lie well.

The first fib you *must* throw out there at the beginning of the date is how early you have to work the next morning. If you really have to work at 9 AM, tell her you have to be there at 8 AM and that you have to wake up at 6:30 AM. This sets your escape plan into action. The time of your blind date should be later in the evening, 8 PM or so. That way you don't arrive at the restaurant at 6 PM and by 7 PM you tell her you have to get to bed soon. Starting at 8 PM allows you to hang out, or suffer, for only two hours, and then tell her you need to get going. If you end up liking her, you can stay out later, or set up a second date with her.

If you don't like your date and she tries to set up another date with you, you must have plans that conflict with whatever date she mentions. The excuses you form can range from having plans with your friends, to having to work during that time. I am not promoting lying for the sake of being deceitful, but rather to save face for your date. The alternative to lying would be to say, "I think you are Chewbacca's sister, and I don't want to go out with you ever." Chances are, if you are on a blind date, you have already exchanged numbers, so the second order of business becomes the "phone dodge". Don't explicitly end the date by telling her you will call her, when you know you won't. This is just a dick move. You kind of have to freestyle and feel out the situation. A tried and true ending is, "OK, it was nice meeting you. Talk to you later." The phone dodge is simply not answering her call or text. Just as you must learn that someone who doesn't answer your calls doesn't want to hang out with you, so she will learn. If you are on your game, during the date you will find out where she is from, and where she hangs out. This is useful information because this is your roadmap for places to stay away from. And conversely, when she asks you where you hang out, you *must* lie, unless you want a stalker. Finally, you need to be ready to be confronted by this girl at some chance meeting at a venue in the future. Make sure you have a reason for not returning her calls. A classic is, "I was going through a lot during that time, and I should have returned your call, but I didn't. I'm sorry." Beautiful. You are humble, pitiful (in a good way), and apologetic. If she asks for specifics, just say that you'd rather not talk about it, or that it's too personal, or a family matter. If she pushes further, she looks like a Nosey Nancy, and she knows this. After your little confrontation, excuse yourself, change location in the venue, or change venues. Do not weak-knee it and tell her you'll call her. This is beneath you, and you owe nothing to anyone.

Listening to a Woman... is it Really Necessary?

Unless you want to be classified as an asshole or a cave dweller, it is imperative to listen to what a woman is saying...sometimes. Women are by nature more talkative and touchy-feely about emotions and ideas. So when their mate is not talkative or emotional, this creates problems. I am not advocating that men discuss last night's *Sex in the City* rerun with their girlfriend, because women also need to recognize that men don't care about women's topics. Men don't get pissed off if women don't want to discuss last night's baseball game, so there needs to be a mutual understanding that there are some things that each gender does not want to listen to.

As far as meeting someone for the first time, instead of thinking about what you're going to say next in the conversation, carefully listen to what the woman is saying to you. Try to remember two pieces of specific information she reveals as she is talking. A little bit later in conversation, ask her about the items you have been remembering. Let's say she told you that she grew up in Chicago with a little brother. Talk about Chicago for a while, and after some time passes, ask how she and her brother get along. This is a great question because it is open-ended and she realizes that you were listening, when she spoke of her brother ten minutes ago. Again, you don't have to record everything she says in your memory, just a couple of things. The things you remember will outshine what you forget or gloss over. When you repeat what she told you minutes ago, it has the subconscious effect of causing her to think that you and her share similar experiences or common ground.

Marriage and the "Taken Girl"

We don't have total control over the timing when we will meet our soul mate. Fate brings us the menu, but we select what we eat. It is a very real possibility that our soul mate made a bad choice and married before she met us. Should marriage be a prison sentence escapable only by the death of one's spouse? Maintaining a marriage just for the sake of the institution itself is a fruitless, miserable endeavor. Working through problems, especially if children exist, goes without saying. All relationships must endure difficult periods, and are a true test of the relationship's durability. The case I am alluding to is a marriage that is miserable, where there are many more difficult times than pleasurable ones. This would also be a marriage with a real disconnect between husband and wife. I am not advocating marrying someone and just staying with him/her until you can "upgrade." That would be insincere and heartless. If you are truly happy in your marriage, you don't need worry about your spouse upgrading, because you've given her no reason to. If she thinks she's with the best, further man-shopping is a waste of her time. She will proudly wear her ring, like a badge of honor.

The case of the "taken" girl, or girl with a boyfriend, at first appears less morally dicey, but on second glance is more complicated than the married woman. At least with a ring, the woman has her cards on the table. Unfortunately, or fortunately, unmarried women don't announce their availability through any outward marking. I have met many unmarried women who are more faithful to their boyfriends than some married women, with rings, are to their husbands. The single man must understand a few principles before approaching the apparently single woman. First off, the woman may be unhappy in her current relationship, and you might very well be the necessary impetus for her to discard her insipid boyfriend. This is why the unhappy girl will likely withhold her availability status, initially. If you repulse her, she can pull out the boyfriend card, and nobody's feelings are hurt. However, if you pique her interest, she may want to explore you some more, as she may want to upgrade from her current situation. Her interest level in you is directly proportional to how you stack up with her current and past suitors. She may try you out for a night, literally in some cases, and decide from there. A key point to remember here is that some single girls are looking for a fling, and if it develops into something more, great, if not, it was a great night anyway.

It seems as though society looks down on flings and random hook-ups. Some view the participants as immature. While a fling can involve two, immature people who make a poor decision that night, two mature adults can successfully pull it off. They are independent people who do not require traditional, dependent relationships to justify their time together. What is the difference if someone sleeps with her suitor on the first date or the tenth? The only difference is that by the time the tenth date occurs, more money and time have been spent, nothing more. If you emotionally connect with someone the night you meet her, why wait weeks before hooking up? One reason this waiting period is ingrained in us is because a woman is seen as "easy" or "cheap" if she hooks up on the first encounter. This is nonsense. So if we follow this logic, then at what date number, or what dollar amount, is it OK to sleep with someone? Date #3? Date #8? I would argue that this is analogous to a hooker who charges $300 per encounter, looking disdainfully at a hooker who only charges $20. The hooker who charges $300 should have no more respect than the $20 hooker. Spending more money or time with someone does not make her more special. She is either special or she is not. Yes, she can grow on you with time, but that is only if you two want to pursue a relationship. If the two of you are mature enough to be honest with each other, a formal relationship is not always necessary. Women that require fancy dinners and gifts before they sleep with a man are nothing more than high-maintenance hookers. Instead of cash, they gladly accept expensive baubles and over-priced nights on the town in exchange for their company.

Just because a person dates around, and is a free spirit, does not make him or her immature. We often hear that "he just needs to settle down, or mature." Having a steady girlfriend or wife is great for some people, but let us not confuse conformity with maturity. Anyone can have a girlfriend or wife. Anyone. There is no skill required to find someone else who does not find you totally repugnant. Until you have found the right person, the mature thing to

31

do is to date around, not settle for what is available. Settling is the sign of immaturity. Usually it is the result of laziness or lowering of expectations. If you date one hundred women and none of them are the "one", you should not say "well, I've dated one hundred women, and that's enough, so I'll settle for the best one out of the hundred." You may need to date one thousand women before you meet the "one". It is a time-consuming process, and it can be frustrating, but no more frustrating than settling on someone, and later meeting the "one".

I would like to make a distinction between settling and settling down. When I use the term "settling", I am referring to the premature surrender to societal pressure to have a wife or girlfriend just for the sake of it. This behavior is pathetic. "Settling down," on the other hand, is a respectable, laudable endeavor. Settling down means that you have found the "one" and are ready to spend your lives together. The hunt is over, and you both have won the game of life. This is the ultimate goal you hope to achieve, after the hard work you've put into improving yourself, and interviewing the many candidates you consider spending your life with.

The Help

There is an old proverb that goes something like this: "Don't fuck the help." Well, sometimes proverbs are helpful, but in this case we'll disregard the warning. "Wow, that waitress/bartender/stripper is hot!" you are thinking. Down, boy! Don't you think that if you are thinking this, 90% of the guys in the venue think the same thing? True, most of these men have vaginas, and are afraid to talk to the girl, but there are some ballsy guys in the club that will try. Don't be one of them. These girls look good, dress the part, and act like they are interested for a reason...your money. If your waitress looked great but acted like a bitch, her tip might not be as stout as it would be if she laughed at your lame jokes and comments. Let's not forget the mechanics of the pick-up are stacked against you. You have only a few seconds to demonstrate your worth to her, or make her demonstrate hers. How do you plan on doing this? Ordering a beer, and then telling her she looks nice, or reminds you of a movie star? Not exactly a great tactical move. This girl has her pick of the litter, and chances are she isn't going to pick a customer who she's interacted with for a total of 5 minutes. Before you get invested, remember that a hired hand is difficult to trust as a girlfriend, because she is constantly the center of attention at work, and interacts with so many people. Quantity has a lot to do with hooking up, and meeting people. If you work in an office, how many new people are you exposed to daily? Now, imagine working in a club. How many people do you think she is exposed to? She has an unlimited number of applications coming in, and she can set up as many interviews as she likes, so to speak.

That being said, hired hands need loving too. There is a very slim, but possible chance of scoring with their kind. It helps if you are a regular, because this helps the girl establish some sort of security. You're not an axe-murderer, and she knows your name is Joe. You can't be the guy at the end of the bar, by yourself either, though. That is not attractive, so you must be lively and have friends there. Throw a few comments her way each week, but do not fawn over her or try to engage her in deep conversation. As time goes on, you may suggest a party or event coming up that she should go to. Do not ask her out. This is not the third grade. If she sounds interested, you could suggest that you get her number and tell her that you and your friends are going, and she (and her friends if she wants) can meet up with you guys, if she wants. This keeps the pressure off of her because you're not asking her to commit to you or a formal date. You two will just happen to be at the same venue together. What happens there will determine if a relationship develops. If she turns down your request for her number, take it like a man and don't beg or act disappointed. There is a reason she is not giving you her number; she doesn't like you, or she is not ready to give it to you yet. If you get the number and she doesn't show up at the venue you suggested, again, don't whine about it or act disappointed. Just talk about what a great time it was, and the new people you met. Don't ever say, "Maybe next time." You invited her once, and she dogged you, so how pathetic is it to invite her a second time? She will likely tell you some excuse why she couldn't make it. Your job in this case? Not caring that she didn't make it. The least she could have done was call or text you to let you know she wouldn't make it. Besides keeping your dignity, the careless attitude you portray will keep things from getting awkward. If you are a regular at the bar and she is the bartender, the last thing you need is for either of you to feel weird around each other or mad.

"The Multiple" and Soul Mates

Another topic rarely discussed outside of confidantes, is that of "the multiple." Quite simply, the multiple is dating more than one person simultaneously. Some look down on this practice, but if you are confident, there is nothing to fear. The "multiple" principle is especially useful for the novice. Are you looking for a soul mate or a sole to mate with? When you are young, it is a waste of time and resources to focus on one person for long periods of time. There is an entire world of people out there, and you have only met the few that reside in your town, bar, or have randomly intersected your life! Do you really think you've found your soul mate from such a small sample? Rarely, yes. Some high school sweethearts are meant for each other. But remember the earlier discussion about a spouse or girlfriend wandering or looking for an upgrade. The remedy to this is simple: **your soul mate has to have life experience.** The high school cheerleader marries the high school quarterback because he's popular, good-looking and she thinks she loves him. Well, she didn't consider that her sample size of suitors was small. He was popular and good-looking compared to the 500 people in the high school. But she didn't consider that popularity only applies in high school and Hollywood, and the moment they graduate, he is no longer the cool quarterback. Is he intelligent? Does he have motivation, or passion? If they stay put in a small town, this may shelter her enough to keep her expectations low. However, if she travels outside her town, or if a suitor crosses her path, the truth will be painfully obvious. There is a lot of "talent" out there, so grabbing the first thing that comes by is ill advised. The oft-quoted line, "if you love something, let it go, and if it comes back it is love" is a poignant reminder of how things work. If you meet and fall for someone with little "relationship experience" (age sometimes correlates with experience, but not always) don't cash in all of your chips immediately. Both of you need to date other people. There should be no fear in losing this person, because if she/he's more attracted to someone else, you've both learned a valuable lesson and avoided future problems of her/him straying from you. If you are indeed soul mates, after sufficient dating around, you will both see that there is nothing better, and you will reunite. This ties in to the principle of multiples as well. At first blush, dating more than one person seems scandalous. It can be tricky, but if done correctly, it is invaluable. The cream always rises to the top with multiples. It should only take one or two dates to decide who, among the multiples, is a keeper. Women date multiples as well; so don't think that only sloven men are guilty. The principle of multiples is *not* long-term dating of multiple people. Not only is long-term dating expensive, but deceit is usually necessary, and is distasteful to all involved. Think of multiples more like a fast-paced rose ceremony from the Bachelor.

III. Essential Topics and Observations in the Dating Scene

The Girl That Fell Off
the Face of the Earth

So you met this great girl, thought you really hit it off, exchanged numbers, and she won't answer or return your calls. Maybe she fell down the stairs and is in the hospital without her cell phone. Not likely. It is usually one of two things when this occurs. The first explanation is that she was drunk when she met you, and she is having second thoughts. Maybe you were *too* smooth or *too* aggressive now that she thinks about it. You were OK at midnight, in a dark bar, with her friends around, but the more she thinks about it, she's not sure about her judgment now. This is the morning-after, cold feet phenomenon. The second explanation of why she's hard to get a hold of is that she is gaming you. She is playing the classic game of "hard-to-get". She wants to see how many times you will call, or how long you will pursue her. This could be to pad her ego, or she could just be doing it because her friends and Cosmo magazine tell her that's how it's done.

Age Differences

Although age is a factor in dating and mating, there are much more important factors to consider. It is hard enough finding a decent human being without the societal pressures of the person having to be about the same age as you. It is true that the closer in age a couple are, the more they will have in common; they will have lived through similar world events, popular music, movie references, etc. That being said, just because two people are close in age, does not mean that they share any similar interests. I enjoy alternative music and comedians who people my own age have never heard of, while some people older (and some younger) have. So age is not an absolute. Age is most important around the legal drinking age. If you are dating someone who is 19 or 20 years old, the venues available for date destinations will be very limited. If your mate isn't of drinking age yet, you're relegated to the movies, dinner and other venues that will quickly grow tiring. You won't be able to go to a happy hour after work for a drink, nor could you get a late night drink after dinner. Bars are almost a necessity, especially early in the relationship. They're nice because the atmosphere is relaxed, you can both "people watch" together, and there's not the pressure to always be carrying on a meaningful conversation. Bars are cheap, impromptu date venues that are great for filling gaps between expensive or formal dates (dinner, museums, opera, etc.). So the bottom line is: make sure she is of age, or has a fake i.d.

If the age difference is too great, the relationship will end quickly because you will be at different stations in your life. If you are 40 years old, and your girlfriend is 21 you may have some great times together, but you are looking toward retirement, while she is looking toward her next party. It will get old. This is why women marry at a younger age than men. Their biological clock does not afford them the opportunity to wait around to settle down and have children.

More important than chronological age is emotional age or maturity. This very topic is the reason I wrote this book. There are some women in their 30's and 40's who still behave like they are in high school. They follow all the silly girl "rules" like making the man spend lots of money on them, making him chase them, etc. And at the other end of the spectrum, there are some 20-year-olds with more emotional maturity than women double their age. These women are straightforward, know what they want, and don't resort to watching "Sex in the City" for life pointers. Trying to find this girl is a life-long mission, because she is not going to knock on your door and introduce herself. She must be sought after. You must search for her, cut through some of her defense mechanisms, and throw yourself out there. If you keep casting, you will eventually catch something (hopefully non-venereal).

The Attention-Magnet
and her Fat-Watcher

There is another kind of woman to be on the lookout for. This woman may be the beauty of the bar, but not necessarily. The woman I am speaking of is the attention-magnet. She loves it when men approach her, and she may even be nice, but she is just out to be admired and on the receiving end of free drinks. She's not sure how to handle someone sincere because she attracts, and is used to, meatheads and pricks. Her behavior is initially cordial, but quickly digresses, as she gets further into conversation. In a way, she is a red herring. She dresses the part and likes the approach, but that's where it ends. Approaching her is like approaching a cardboard cutout of Jessica Alba. Sure, the cutout catches your eye, but that only lasts for so long. This girl has spent so much time cultivating her exterior that she has neglected her interior. She has the designer bag, Seven jeans, a $200 hairstyle, and a void where there could be a personality. Usually, this woman travels with a couple other women so she can seek their approval before she commits to conversation with another adult. This usually requires a bathroom break for the girls to "discuss". God forbid she makes a decision as an individual, without the council of her peers. You should depart this woman's company as soon as she goes to council in the bathroom.

So who comprises a woman's council? It could be a good friend or two. Or it could be women she doesn't see as competition. This increases her odds of success, and if she is even slightly more attractive than her friends, she looks even better when standing next to them. Vanilla ice cream looks great. But put it next to a scoop of vanilla ice cream with chocolate syrup, whipped cream and a cherry on it, and I'd eat the shit out of the latter. The woman's intentions aren't always to one-up her friends, but this is often the end result. Since the most attractive woman receives all the attention, the less attractive friends become jealous, and try to shoot down any incoming men approaching the hot woman. One of my good friends, C.S., aptly named these spoilers, or haters, "fat-watchers" because they monitor or "watch" the woman you are interested in. Their weight isn't a requisite for the title, but if they are not obese then they are unattractive, lesbian or old. Diplomacy is required when dealing with their type. If you don't have a friend ("wingman") to run interference or "take one for the team" for you, you have your hands full. **Never ignore the fat-watcher!** She is the gatekeeper. If she hates you, she will tell her attractive friend to shut you down. And in packs, women care more about each other's feelings than hooking up with "some strange". If you ignore the fat-watcher, her friend will feel bad that the "watcher" is sitting all alone. The "watcher" must be greased like a dirty politician, but in place of money, you will use conversation and listening to disarm her. So, involve her in the conversation and/or the drinks you buy. If the fat-watcher likes you, you've just picked up an ally. You also look like a gentleman in front of the girl you are pursuing. If the fat-watcher becomes *too* interested in you, and the one you're pursuing doesn't save you, you need to get out of there before the watcher asks for your number. It is very awkward to lie about why you can't give your number out. If you give the wrong number on purpose, just remember that you may come back to that bar someday and run into the fat-watcher again.

It is worth noting that a "fat-watcher" can also be a gay, male friend of the woman. The rules for engaging the watcher are the same: involve him in conversation, buy him drinks, etc. Be very wary of a woman whose best friend is a gay man, though. You need to find out why her best friend isn't a member of her own sex. Would a guy have a girl as a best friend? No. So, it's not a deal-breaker if her friend is gay, but proceed with caution.

Forbidden Dance

Not "the Forbidden Dance" as in the Lambada, but "dance is forbidden"… if you have testicles. John Ashcroft and the Baptists have it right when they say that dancing is a sin. There are some ground rules gentlemen should observe, with regard to dancing. 1) Dancing is only acceptable when a woman is involved, and specifically, when she invites you. 2) Under no circumstances should a man venture to the dance floor solo, or with a buddy. This behavior is acceptable only if you want to look like George Michael and his partner from Wham, or if you're a homo-gay. 3) If a woman calls you out to the dance floor, you must report for duty. And do not forget that the dance floor is not the place for you to experiment with moves you saw in an Usher video the day before. 4) Keep it low-key and minimal.

Cougar Hunting

Just as all felines come out at night to hunt, so do the "cougars". "Cougar" is the popular term for older (usually 35 or older) women out on the town looking for some young meat. Think hot, divorced soccer mom. These women have been around the block, so they don't play the same childish games that some younger women play. The reason for this is because the cougars are at, or just past, their prime and they don't have time for games. They know what they want, and they pursue it. A cougar is a bird in the hand for any young man. He doesn't have to decode too many signals from her; nor does he have to buy her dinner or call her every day to check in. Usually, the cougar is a cat looking for a play toy, and if the man is game, both parties are satisfied.

The best places to go cougar hunting are wine bars and jazz bars. These places tend to attract an older crowd, and if you are one of the few young men in the place, you will stand out in a good way. Cougars tend to shy away from the hippest dance clubs and bars because the crowd is so much younger. The cougar would really appear out of place in the young club, especially if she tried to use some of the dance moves from her youth. So, while a younger man can assimilate in an older demographic bar, the converse is true for the woman. They stand out like sore thumbs in younger bars, and people start asking whose mother is at the bar. The other reason cougars tend to skip the younger bars is because of the competition. They know that most young men will be more attracted to a girl in her twenties than to a woman approaching forty. This is another reason why it is easier to pick up a cougar than a younger woman. The cougar knows that she does not have her pick of the litter, and if she blows you off, another suitor may not approach her that night.

Critics

As you maneuver through life and mingle with the opposite sex, you will earn a reputation. It is said that your character is what you really are, while your reputation is what others think you are. So it is all a matter of perception, really. If someone heard a rumor (false or true) about you, they create your reputation based on the information that they are presented. At this point, it should be glaringly obvious that you cannot possibly control the information about you that is disseminated to the masses. So don't worry about the masses. Focus on a select few, and shape their perceptions of you favorably. Is this manipulative? Yes. But everyone is manipulating someone at all times. You manipulate people just by smiling at them. You are trying to engage them, or change their state by your smile. You buy your friends and family gifts at Christmas. If you didn't, don't you think they would view you as strange? You are manipulating their view of you. Our conformity to society REQUIRES that we manipulate others. What do you think marketing and advertising are? Mere tools of manipulation. The point is that manipulation is not necessarily a bad thing. Again, select the target you are interested in, and market yourself. As spectators watch and judge you, are you cheesy, bold, or, God forbid, different acting as you try to pick up a woman? It doesn't matter because we have our eye on the prize, and the spectators can fuck themselves if they don't like us. After all, we're not trying to pick up the spectators. If the woman digs you, you're in. It's that simple. This is the very reason why trying to look cool and not smile is lame. You look like every other asshole in the place that doesn't want to take a chance to be different or original. I actually prefer it when guys try to act cool, because this means less competition for me. What a different scene it would be if everyone in the bar was genuine, funny, and engaging! The next time you go out to a social setting like a bar, look around and take note how many people interact with you. You will find the number can usually be counted on the hand of a 3-fingered man. People are afraid to interact, and when you engage them, they are bewildered at what is going on. It is refreshing when I talk to a woman, and don't immediately compliment her looks, or offer her a drink. She is so used to the same old ritual, that she is truly befuddled when she is not fawned over. This is the secret. This approach challenges her dominant position. No longer is she on a pedestal to be admired and drinks purchased for her. Rather, she is now an equal, and must prove her worth to you, just as you must prove your worth to her.

Posers, Posturers, and Pathetics

Everyone has seen these busters, who pose and posture before the ladies in an effort to camouflage their lack of confidence. The telltale sign of these guys is their face. They will never look amiable if they pass another man. They will display one of three faces, the "I don't see anyone", the "tough guy", or the "hi, fuck you" face.

The "I don't see you" face is the absolute weakest of the three faces because they are afraid to make eye contact with another guy. They will look past you, as if to say, "I am near-sighted and don't see anyone I'm not talking to." A fun way to mess with these guys is to move into the space they are staring away at. If they are looking just to your left, move left. It's comical to be able to control someone's head like an oscillating fan without saying a word.

The "tough guy" face is also the "no smile" or even a pissed off look, like someone just stole his last syringe of "the juice." For all three of these guys, it's not cool for them to be friendly or say "hi" to another passing guy, but "tough guy" wants you to know he's not gay, so he'll look at you, but won't acknowledge you. This is the same guy that pushes his way through a crowd without saying, "excuse me." He's confused himself with Moses, and he assumes everyone will part like the Red Sea, so he can pass. And if you don't move out of his way, he'll front, and try to stare you down. As you laugh at this bag of douche, he'll ask if you have a problem. Say, "yes," and then tell him about your life's problems: credit, girls, that rash you can't get rid of, etc. He will really appreciate your levity.

Finally, the "hi, fuck you" guy is also the "single-nodder." He sees you, throws his nose up and his head back, ala a West Coast rapper. This would be the same greeting an ex-boyfriend would give his girl's current boyfriend if they passed each other in a club. Essentially, his Tourette-style head-flip says, "Hey, fuck you."

The aforementioned characters lack confidence, and outwardly manifest it. There are other men that aren't so obvious. They may wear a pink polo shirt, as if to scream that they're the definition of confidence, but the rest of the world knows that only two classes of men are allowed to wear pink shirts: married men and gay men. Brass balls are not equivalent to self-confidence either. Most of the time brass balls equate to delusion. The classic example of this is the thug, or douche trying to be a thug, approaching women. These guys are wearing wife-beaters, gold chains, hat sideways, and over-sized clothing usually branded with sports logos or FUBU. They don't have a career, secondary schooling, ambition, or a clue. I am not suggesting that a man needs a college degree to be successful or a decent human being, but living and dressing like a hoodlum is unacceptable. Most of the time, they still live in their mother's house. They are too stupid to realize they are approaching another *species* of human and are truly out of their league. They act totally confident, but it is literally an act, replete with their silly costume and thug accent. These thespians don't have a handle on their own life and are

43

without a station in life. They *want* to be confident, the same way they *want* to be feared as a thuggish *gangsta*. Just because they approach every lady they encounter, does not mean they are confident. Lack of self-awareness and propriety is not confidence. One could go out tomorrow and tell 100 people he's Jesus Christ. Most normal people would know that he is not Jesus, and the guy is full of shit. The same thing happens when our fake-confidence thug approaches his woman target. Within minutes, his game crumbles like a cookie, as she asks him what he does for a living, where he lives, and what his interests are. "Circuit City, mom's basement, and fucking women" usually doesn't bode well as a response.

Expectations and "being a dick"

You've got your hair gelled just right, your clothes are looking good, and you're ready to hit the town. But before you walk out the door, you've got some mental preparation to do. Some guys think that their night is successful if they take a woman home, or at least her number. Anyone conforming to this frat-boy litmus test is in for a miserable life. First of all, every night you go out, you are not going to score. Does this mean you failed? That depends on what your expectations were. If your goal is to score a girl or number every time you go out, then going out is like a job, and you are acting like a 9-to-5 corporate chump in a conference room, who measures his success with measurable, obtainable goals. Who wants his happiness predicated on someone else's acceptance of him? This type of person is only happy if a stranger gives him her body or number; otherwise, his night is shot to hell. The best attitude to adopt each night is confident indifference, or as those who don't understand it call it, "being a dick". You are confident in how you look, what you stand for, and how you carry yourself. Any woman would be foolish to not be attracted to this. And this indifference means that you are going to have a good time, regardless if you talk to or connect with a woman that night. You are showing that you are not a desperate newbie who will salivate over anything that looks his way. Sure, if you are getting a vibe from a woman, you will approach her. But if you don't get a vibe from anyone that night, that is OK too. You are not saying you are better than everyone, but you are making a statement that you're comfortable enough with yourself that you don't have to hook-up to prove your worth.

Not every venue is going to present you with opportunity. Some venues are going to be "talent-less". That being said, you may go to a venue that is "talent-laden", and the women want nothing to do with you. This doesn't mean you failed, but maybe you are having an off night, or the women are not right for you. Managing expectations is so important because it is easy to become depressed or frustrated when you have a sub-par night. A hackneyed, but poignant metaphor is the baseball player who is hitting .300. This is a great batting average, but if someone who didn't understand baseball saw this average, they may conclude, correctly, the player failed two out of three times. It is all about perspective. And finally, let's discuss luck. The Seneca quote that "luck is when preparation meets opportunity" is timeless. This book, and your work toward self-improvement, takes care of the preparation portion of the equation. As for the opportunity, that is up to fate. Never forget that there are many people who have been blessed with intelligence, looks, and money, and failed. All the preparation and talent in the world, is useless if there is no opportunity to apply it. A person can have the greatest idea for an invention, or even a book, but if they are not presented the opportunity, they will not achieve their goal. The best you can do is to prepare and pray the stars align.

Proper Interaction with Other Men

Our interactions with other men can be just as important as our interactions with women. If a woman sees us acting arrogant or intimidated by another man, our stock falls immediately in her eyes. But more than just impressing her, we should be able to carry ourselves as gentleman for our own peace of mind.

When you accidentally bump into another guy or need to reach past him for a drink, a polite, "Excuse me," or "I'm sorry, bud," is in order. How many times have you wanted to destroy the asshole, who bumps into you while you were just minding your own damn business and standing still? Then he looks at you as if you should have cleared a path for him, as if he were Christ. So that you don't come off as an asshole, is only one reason why you should exercise manners with other guys. Another reason is that it is the right thing to do, and the world would be a better place if everyone were more courteous. That being said, the chump who bumps you and stares you down needs to be stood up   to … usually. If you are on a date, and this confrontation will ruin it, then it is definitely not worth your time. But if you are at a bar or concert, it is not a serious date, and some prick disrespects you, you need to stand your ground, literally. If a guy does not say, "Excuse me," but tries to walk through me, I don't budge. I look at him and laugh at his lack of manners. He usually gets pissed and lippy, at which point I continue laughing and tell him that if he wanted me to move, all he had to do was say the magic words that his mommy taught him when he was a little boy. If you don't stand up to these guys, they don't learn, and you look like a little bitch for moving out of their way because they want you to.

And now for the softer side of man/man interactions. No, not like that. You should go out of your way to talk to other guys at the places you hang out. One reason for this is that it will diffuse situations before they arise. For instance, as you are waiting for your drink at the bar, you say something funny to one of the guys at the bar. Now, for the rest of the night, he knows that you are a cool guy. The next time you go up to get a drink, he'll clear the way for you, because he knows you. Or if some guy is being a jerk to you, your new friend may know this guy and tell him to stop bothering you. Another reason why you should be cool with other guys is because it exudes confidence. No, you're not afraid to talk to guys because people might think you're gay. Gayness is only if you try to pick up guys or tell them how nice they look in jeans. When you talk to other guys, you are showing the entire room that you are so comfortable with yourself that you can talk to anyone.

I would be remiss if I didn't mention the subject of friends. Be very careful with your friends and women you introduce them to. Some very good friends are capable of very bad things. I speak from experience. Your friends are human and have the same sexual drive you have, so don't think for a minute that they just turn it off when you bring your girl around. All it takes is for you to walk away for a minute, and the guy will find a reason why he needs the girl to give him her number. And it always sounds innocent, never overt. Maybe he asks for her number, "just in case he needs to reach her." Usually, these are casual friends that pull this, not your best friends, although they're not outside the realm of possibility. I mentioned earlier the situation of the "taken girl", or the girl with a boyfriend. This girl has a boyfriend, but he may be a douche bag, and she just now met you, a great guy. Is it unethical to approach her? That depends on your values and morals. I absolutely don't seek out attached women, nor do I turn them away...unless they are involved with my good friend. I only have a few, very good friends, and I respect their friendship so much, that no matter how hot their girlfriend is, or what she says, there is no doubt in my mind that she is off limits. My rule of thumb is this: if know the guy she is with, I'll stay away; if I don't know her guy, and she is showing interest in me, then all's fair. I don't owe any allegiance to a guy that I don't even know. The girl can be the judge of who is better, him or me. Some of my friends argue that it doesn't matter if you know the guy or not; you should stay away. I respectfully disagree.

Ex-Lovers

Exes are a topic that surfaces over and over again throughout life. What is proper etiquette if you see an ex? Can you be friends? Can you trust your lover to spend time with an ex for "drinks"? Ex-lovers do not have to be a complicated issue, as long as the parties involved follow the same rules with regard to their exes. If you are a smart man, you will have learned to never burn bridges, no matter how vile your ex was. Scorned women will sully your reputation to other women, and any chance encounters with these exes will be particularly awkward. Treat women as you would treat a business client, for word of mouth can make or break your social status. On the occasion when you do run into an ex, don't look away, or act like you don't see her. This is cowardly, and beneath you. There is no reason to cower, as long as you haven't burned any bridges. Say "hello", and ask something innocuous such as work, or how she has been doing, but keep it brief. It is best that you end the conversation, and tell her you must go; otherwise you look like a fool who wants to catch up on the details of her life. You don't care, so don't waste time talking to her. Don't ask her if she is seeing anyone. It makes you look nosey, and she will be defensive anyway, feeling that you are comparing who has done better since you parted ways.

Men and women cannot be friends, unless one of the parties has no physical attraction to the other. As humans, we are hard-wired to reproduce, so sex is always in our head (whether you are conscious of it or not). Just look at the animal kingdom for proof. Do male frogs and female frogs just "hang out" for camaraderie? No. They make babies, because this is what males and females do, regardless of the animal. Humans have the same instincts, and they cannot just turn them off on a whim.

If you are dating a woman, and one of your exes calls you to hang out, you must choose wisely. Since at one time you had a relationship with your ex, you must have found her attractive, at least at some point. Therefore, your current lover should not look favorably to you putting yourself in a tempting situation. Women are notorious for this. "Yes, we used to date, but now we're just friends. Nothing's going on; he's just a friend now." Sound familiar? While there are a few, truly naïve women who actually believe this, the rest of them are just being duplicitous, thinking they can fool you with these lines. These women also attack you if you even question who this guy is, or when they dated. Women like to throw the word "insecure" your way if you have an issue with them "hanging out" with an ex. There is nothing good that can come out of your woman going out with an ex. The only exception, is if he has recently come out of the closet, and thus, no longer sexually interested in your woman. Other than that, why would a guy want to "hang out" with his ex-girlfriend? Clearly, at one time, both parties were attracted to each other. Over time, one of the parties broke off the relationship. Usually both parties don't agree at the exact same moment to end the relationship, so the question becomes, "who ended the relationship?" The point is moot for you, because one of the two parties was still interested in the other, when the other broke off the relationship. So, maybe initially, the ex-boyfriend thought she was hot, they hooked up a few times, she discovered she didn't like him, and dumped him. Sure, he tells her he wants to be friends. He thinks if he hangs around long enough, he could garner redemption. And let's remember, he still thinks she's hot, whether she dumped him or not.

And let's not forget "fuck-buddies". Such a dirty connotation for such a great, no-strings-attached relationship. This relationship is great because both parties are enjoying themselves without the drama of a typical relationship. You don't have to go out for expensive dinners, you both have your freedom, and you don't have to call to check in every day to prove your love. Fuck-buddies are typically exes who may or may not be in a new relationship. The half-life of a fuck-buddy pair is typically short, because one of the two eventually wants more in a relationship than sex. The existence of a fuck-buddy is one of the main reasons never to throw out a phone number. You never know when fate will smile upon you in the future. The custom for this relationship is that one of the two "buddies" has had a little bit too much to drink and texts or calls the other person. The hookup develops from that fateful call.

Values and Why Women and Men Fight

It is easy to see how values will affect the suitor looking for a mate: If "fun" is at the top of his hierarchy, he may go out looking to "bed women", instead of "wed" them. Typically, this guy would be labeled a bachelor or player. If he has "love" ranked higher than "fun", chances are he is looking for a connection, or lasting relationship with a woman. He's not interested in the one-night stand, and usually this guy has a serious girlfriend or is married.

Most people I've met don't even think about their value hierarchy. Consequently, these same people are shocked when their lover doesn't return phone calls, cheats on them, or treats them poorly. If the girl or guy hasn't called you in two days, does it mean that he/she is blowing you off? This could be the case, or it could be that this person is totally comfortable having a friend or lover that he calls once or twice a week. If you are the type who needs to talk to your friends/lovers every day, you may mistakenly think the rare-caller doesn't value your friendship. An outsider can clearly see that there is a mismatch of communication styles between the two, but the rare-caller may be confused why his friend/lover is acting strangely when he *does* call, or why she is acting mad or busy. Unless she understands his values (not needing to call every day), or he understands hers (would like daily contact), the relationship is doomed. And this example is just in the area of the telephone! Imagine how many other communication-style mismatches can occur: guy talking to other girls (and vice-versa), guy wanting to hang out with the guys (instead of her *all* of the time), etc. The differences in men and women's hierarchies are the same reason men don't want to get married right away (or at all), and women do. Most men value freedom and fun over commitment, whereas women value relationships and commitment more. If the woman wants marriage, she needs to find a man who is at the same emotional maturity level, and the same decision-making crossroad. If the woman is twenty-five years old and wants to have a few children in her future, she is pressuring (not necessarily a bad pressure) herself to find a stable man. She then, in turn, pressures her boyfriend to commit. Some twenty one year old men are capable and willing to settle down and get married, although I would argue that most are not. As the man ages, he usually draws closer to the decision making crossroad of commitment. The disconnect that happens between couples is that the woman reaches this crossroad years before the man. She wants a ring, but he's not sure. Despite what we keep hearing about how the man *needs* to pop the question after X amount of months or years of dating, if he is not at the same decision-making crossroad, he should not commit. Commitment is serious business, and there is no formula for when he needs to commit by. Men tend to be more timid with regard to marriage because of a simple economic principle that many of these same men probably haven't even heard of. It is an economic principle known as the Law of Diminishing Returns, which states that each additional unit of input yields progressively less and less additional output. An example of this would be if you eat one or two pieces of pizza, you are satisfied, but if you eat 10 pieces, your enjoyment declines with each subsequent piece. This relates to social interactions in that when men meet and date a woman for a week or two, things are great. But the longer he dates her, the less enjoyment he gains (if she is not the one, of course). That being said, if he really loves this woman and can see himself growing old with her, he should seriously consider her ultimatum. He needs to decide if he is just not ready, or if she is not the "one." It would be shame for him to let the "one" get away because he can't make up his mind if he wants to settle down or play the field some more. The man should know if she is the "one" within a few months at the most. By that time, you should have spent a lot of time together and discussed your thoughts on how you see your future (where to live, if you want kids, religion, etc.).

The bottom line is to find someone with similar value rankings to your own. Couples talk about finances and children before they tie the knot, but all too often they fail to discuss value hierarchies. A person, who ranks his career above his wife or family, will have a difficult time with his marriage if his wife expects to be in the #1 slot and his career in the #2 slot. This man thinks it is more important for him to put extra hours in at the office, while the wife may view this as his love of work over her. Some people are fine with this arrangement, and it works out great. We've seen the couples that each work more than forty hours per week and hardly see each other during the week. The great amount of time that they spend apart during the week makes the time they spend together on weekends even more special to them. If they saw each other every day for extended periods of time, they may grow tired of each other. Other couples need to eat dinner together every night and need to talk to each other on the phone daily. Every person and couple has unique requirements, and it is up to both individuals to flesh these out at the beginning of the relationship.

Parting Words and Final Thoughts

Hopefully, you've learned a thing or two about women, relationships, or yourself from this book. The suggestions given in this book were taken from personal experience and research, but remember that everything doesn't always work all of the time. You may think you've got a girl all figured out, and then you never see or hear from her again. These are the intangibles, my friend. These are the things that make life such an adventure. The best we can do is to have fun living life, instead of preparing for the life we want to live. It is OK to try, to fail, to laugh, and to love. The road to find our soul mate has a beginning and an end. It is the on the road between these two points that we grow, adapt, and truly discover who we are.

Special Thanks

Thank you to the following people, without whom this book would not be possible. Dan, who has been a dear friend and taught me more about women than I can share. Jeff, Nick, Laura, three of my siblings, sounding boards, proofreaders, and moral support. Chris, for our musings on life and people. CPenn, for the photography and ideas for the book cover. Beth, Natalie, Marie, and Kyle, for being my models for an hour. Brandon, Mike and Steve, for being wingmen as we conducted our field research. Jessie, for inspiring me to figure life out. Howie, at Twist, who graciously allowed us to shoot our cover in his club. And Anthony Robbins, whose books spurred me to investigate social behavior further.

www.ingramcontent.com/pod-product-compliance
Lightning Source LLC
Chambersburg PA
CBHW032035090426
42741CB00006B/823